Symbols of Freedom

National Parks

Denali National Park and Preserve

M.C. Hall

Heinemann Library
Chicago, Illinois

Page layout by Ron Kamen and edesign
Photo research by Maria Joannou and Erica Newbery
Illustrations by Martin Sanders
Printed and bound in China by South China Printing Company Limited

10 09 08 07 06
10 9 8 7 6 5 4 3 2 1

Library of Congress Cataloging-in-Publication Data
Hall, Margaret, 1947-
    Denali National Park and Preserve/ M.C. Hall.
        p. cm. -- (Symbols of freedom)
    Includes bibliographical references and index.
    ISBN 1-4034-7794-9 (library binding - hardcover)
1. Denali National Park and Preserve (Alaska)--Juvenile literature. 2. Natural history--Alaska--Denali National Park and Preserve--Juvenile literature. I. Title. II. Series.
    F912.M23H35 2006
    917.98'3--dc22

                                    2005026569

Acknowledgments
The author and publishers are grateful to the following for permission to reproduce copyright material:
Alamy Images pp. **7** (Richard Broadwell), **10** (Alaska Stock LLC), **14** (Alaska Stock LLC), **19** (Danita Delimont); Corbis pp. **8**, **11** (Galen Rowell), **12** (Alissa Crandall), **15** (Joel W. Rogers), **17**, **18** (George D. Lepp), **20** (Douglas Peebles), **24** (W. Wayne Lockwood, M.D.), **25** (Danny Lehman), **27** (Wolfgang Kaehler); Getty Images pp. **4** (National Geographic/Mark Cosslett), **5** (Photographer's Choice/Johnny Johnson), **16** (Taxi), **22** (Stone), **23** (Image Bank); National Park Service pp. **13**, **26**; Niebrugge Images p. **21**; USGS p. **9**.

Cover photograph of Denali National Park and Preserve reproduced with permission of NHPA/John Shaw.
The Publishers would like to thank Ingrid Nixon, Education Coordinator at Denali National Park and Preserve, for her assistance in the preparation of this book.

Every effort has been made to contact copyright holders of any material reproduced in this book.
Any omissions will be rectified in subsequent printings if notice is given to the publisher.

Some words are shown in bold, **like this**. You can find out what they mean by looking in the glossary.

Contents

Our National Parks

National parks are areas of land for people to visit and enjoy. These parks do not belong to one person. They belong to everyone in the United States.

There are **388** national park areas in the
United States. Denali is one of the largest
parks in the country. The entire state of
Vermont could fit inside the park.

Denali

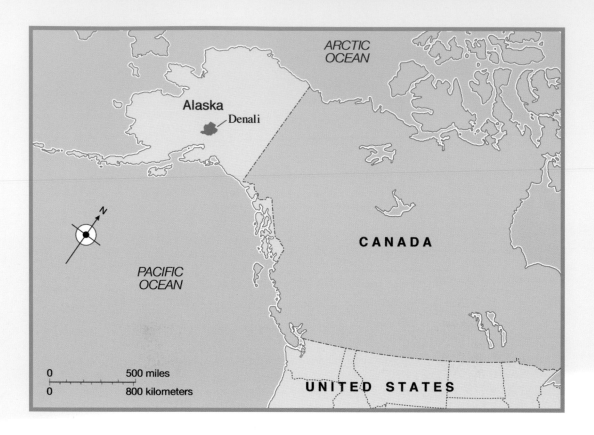

Denali is in Alaska, the largest state in the United States. Alaska is also the most northern state. The country of Canada lies between Alaska and the rest of the United States.

There is a large mountain in the park. The **Athabascan** people of Alaska call it "Denali." In their language, this means "the high one." That is how the park got its name.

The Alaskan Mountain **Range** runs through the park.

Denali Long Ago

The first people to live in Denali were the **Athabascans**. They traveled to the area following the animals that they hunted. A gold rush in 1903 brought more people to the area.

This photo is of an Athabascan family.

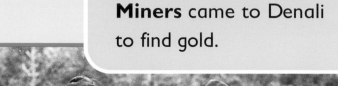

Miners came to Denali to find gold.

People wanted to protect the area's **wildlife**. In 1917, the government created Mt. McKinley National Park. In 1980, the name was changed to Denali National Park and Preserve.

Visiting Denali

Most people visit Denali in the summer. Visitors can hike, camp, fish, watch **wildlife**, and look at the beautiful **scenery**.

In the summer, the days are long.

In the winter, Denali is very cold. The days are short and it is harder to get around the park.

Winter visitors go cross-country skiing and **snowshoeing**.

Getting Around in Denali

Most of Denali is a **wilderness**. Only one road leads there. Some people hike or ride bikes to places they want to see. However, most people ride on **shuttle buses**.

Most visitors do not drive cars through the park.

The shuttle buses take people all over the park. Visitors can get out to hike and take photographs of the **scenery**. They also try to spot wild animals.

Mt. McKinley

Mt. McKinley is one of the most famous sights in Denali. It is the highest mountain in North America.

Mt. McKinley can be seen from lots of places in the park.

It can take more than three weeks to reach the top.

Experienced climbers sometimes try to climb Mt. McKinley. They use special equipment to climb the icy slopes.

Glaciers

Some parts of the park have many **glaciers**. They form when winter snow does not melt during the summer. The snow packs down and becomes ice. It starts to move slowly down the mountainside.

Some of the glaciers in Denali are huge. Glaciers can be dangerous to walk on. The ice can crack and form a deep opening called a **crevasse**.

This small glacier can be seen from the park road.

Tundra Plants

Much of Denali National Park and Preserve is **tundra**. The tundra is land with no trees. Only small plants can grow there.

In the summer, the top few inches of tundra soil **thaw**. Small bushes, grass, and wildflowers grow in this thin layer of soil.

Other Park Plants

Thick forests of willow and birch trees grow in parts of Denali. As the land gets higher, there are fewer trees. No trees grow at all above **timberline**.

There are no plants at all on the highest mountains. These **peaks** are always covered with snow. Nothing can grow there.

Park Animals

Denali is famous for the big animals that live there. Most visitors hope to spot grizzly bears and wolves. Dall sheep live high in the mountains.

Caribou also live in the park.

Many bears live in Denali. The park is also home to smaller animals like mice, snowshoe hares, ground squirrels, birds, and fish.

Some lucky visitors might see a bear.

Sled Dogs

Denali is also famous for an animal that is not wild. Sled dogs are trained to pull sleds across the snow. Long ago, that was the best way to travel in Alaska.

Visitors like to see the park's sled dogs.

People can visit the dogs in their **kennels**.
They can watch a show that tells them how
sled dogs work. In the winter, **park rangers**
travel around the park by sled dog.

Park Buildings and People

There are two visitor centers in Denali National Park and Preserve. People start their visit at one of the centers. They get information there about the park.

Park rangers work in the visitor centers and in other places around the park. Rangers lead hikes. They also give talks about the **wildlife** and mountains of the park.

Map of Denali

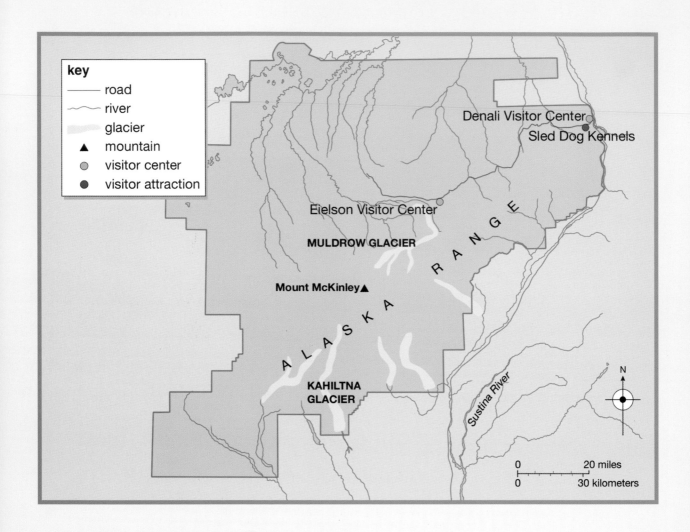

key
road
river
glacier
▲ mountain
visitor center
visitor attraction

Denali Visitor Center
Sled Dog Kennels

Eielson Visitor Center

MULDROW GLACIER

Mount McKinley▲

ALASKA RANGE

KAHILTNA
GLACIER

Sustina River

N

0   20 miles
0   30 kilometers

Timeline

12,000 years ago	Hunters come to Denali area to follow herds of caribou and other animals.
Thousands of years ago	Athabascan people live in the Denali area.
1867	United States buys Alaska from Russia.
1897	The Alaskan Gold Rush starts.
1903	Gold is discovered in Denali.
1910	Three men reach the north peak of Mt. McKinley.
1917	Mt. McKinley National Park is created.
1922	The Alaska Railroad reaches Denali. More visitors begin to come to the park.
1959	Alaska becomes the 49th state of the United States.
1976	Mt. McKinley National Park becomes an International Biosphere Reserve.
1980	The government makes the park much bigger and renames it Denali National Park and Preserve.

Glossary

Athabascan native person of Alaska

crevasse deep crack in ice

glaciers large areas of moving ice and snow

kennel shelter for dogs

miner person who works in a mine

national park natural area set aside by the government for people to visit

park ranger person who works in a national park and shares information about the wildlife and unusual sights of the park

peak highest part of a mountain

range group of mountains

scenery beautiful sights of an area

shuttle bus bus that takes people from place to place and makes stops along the way

snowshoe to travel on top of the snow on snowshoes that are attached to boots

thaw melt

timberline imaginary line beyond which trees cannot grow

tundra flat, frozen land with no trees

wilderness are that is wild and natural

wildlife wild animals of an area

Find Out More

Books

An older reader can help you with these books:

Gibbons, Gail. *Grizzly Bears*. New York, NY: Holiday House, 2003.

Llewellyn, Claire. *Glaciers*. Geography Starts Series. Chicago, IL: Heinemann Library, 2002.

Stone, Lynn M. *America's National Parks*. Land of Liberty Series. Vero Beach, FL: Rourke, 2002.

Address

To find out more about Denali National Park and Preserve, write to:

Denali National Park
P.O. Box 9
Denali Park, AK 99755-0009
Tel: 907-683-2294

Website

You can visit the park's official site at:

http://www.nps.gov/dena

Index